PUBLICATION OF THE AMERICAN DIALECT SOCIETY

Number 21

EASTERN DIALECT WORDS IN CALIFORNIA

By

DAVID W. REED

SUPPLEMENTARY LIST OF
SOUTH CAROLINA WORDS AND PHRASES

By

F. W. BRADLEY

THE SECRETARY'S REPORT

Published by the

AMERICAN DIALECT SOCIETY

April, 1954

Obtainable from the Secretary of the Society

Anderson Hall, University of Florida
Gainesville, Florida

OFFICERS

OF

THE AMERICAN DIALECT SOCIETY

PRESIDENT

JAMES B. McMILLAN   *University of Alabama*

VICE-PRESIDENT

LEVETTE J. DAVIDSON   *University of Denver*

SECRETARY-TREASURER

THOMAS PYLES   *University of Florida*

EDITING COMMITTEE

JAMES B. McMILLAN   *University of Alabama*
I. WILLIS RUSSELL   *University of Alabama*
THE SECRETARY, *ex-officio*

EXECUTIVE COUNCIL

JAMES B. McMILLAN   *University of Alabama*
LEVETTE J. DAVIDSON   *University of Denver*
THOMAS PYLES   *University of Florida*
LORENZO D. TURNER   (term expires Dec., 1954)   *Roosevelt College*
JOSIAH H. COMBS   (term expires Dec., 1955)   *Mary Washington*
                                            College of the University of Va.
MARGARET M. BRYANT (term expires Dec., 1956)   *Brooklyn College*
KARL W. DYKEMA   (term expires Dec., 1957)   *Youngstown College*

CHAIRMEN OF THE RESEARCH COMMITTEES

REGIONAL SPEECH AND LOCALISMS   *Raven I. McDavid, Jr.,*
                                         Western Reserve University
PLACE NAMES   *E. C. Ehrensperger, University of South Dakota*
LINGUISTIC GEOGRAPHY *Albert H. Marckwardt, University of Michigan*
USAGE   *Karl W. Dykema, Youngstown College*
NON-ENGLISH DIALECTS   *Einar Haugen, University of Wisconsin*
NEW WORDS   *I. Willis Russell, University of Alabama*
PROVERBIAL SAYINGS   *Margaret M. Bryant, Brooklyn College*

REGIONAL SECRETARIES

NEW ENGLAND   *B. J. Whiting, Harvard University*
MIDDLE ATLANTIC STATES   *C. K. Thomas, Cornell University*
SOUTH ATLANTIC STATES   *Atcheson L. Hench, University of Virginia*

Continued on Cover 3

PUBLICATION OF THE AMERICAN DIALECT SOCIETY

Number 21

1 2 ?

EASTERN DIALECT WORDS IN CALIFORNIA

By

DAVID W. REED

SUPPLEMENTARY LIST OF
SOUTH CAROLINA WORDS AND PHRASES

By

F. W. BRADLEY

THE SECRETARY'S REPORT

Published by the

AMERICAN DIALECT SOCIETY

April, 1954

Obtainable from the Secretary of the Society

Anderson Hall, University of Florida
Gainesville, Florida

EASTERN DIALECT WORDS IN CALIFORNIA

DAVID W. REED

University of California, Berkeley

The student of California dialects must take into careful account the unusual, often unique, patterns of California settlement history. The most striking fact about that history is the unparalleled rate of growth of the population. In the 1850 census, the first in which California participated, the population of the state was found to be over 92,000,[1] and a large share of that number had entered during the Gold Rush of the preceding year. In 1860 the population was found to have increased at the phenomenal rate of 360 per cent to a figure of almost 380,000. Although this rate of increase was never again attained, the proportion of increase by decades has never fallen below 20 per cent. The percentage increase in the depression years of the 1930's was 21, and in the 1890's it was 22. On the other hand it reached 60 between 1900 and 1910, 65 between 1920 and 1930, and 53 between 1940 and 1950. In the 93 years since 1860, the population of California has doubled, on an average, every 18 years; and the rate of growth shows no sign of slacking. With the 1950 census, California surpassed Pennsylvania, to become the second most populous state in the Union.

Even more startling than the growth of the state as a whole is the rate of increase of California urban population. Between 1850 and 1860 the urban population grew from 6,820 to over 78,000— an increase of 1053 per cent! The proportion of the state's population that was urban in 1860 amounted to less than 21 per cent. By 1950, four out of five of the state's ten and one-half million people lived in cities of more than 5,000 inhabitants. At the same time, vast areas of California mountains and desert were among the most sparsely settled regions in the country.

Coincident with the growth of cities has been a shift in the population center from the San Francisco Bay area to Southern

---

[1] The population statistics here and in what follows are taken from the following publications of the U. S. Bureau of the Census: *Seventh Census of the United States* (1850), through *Seventeenth Census of the United States* (1950). The titles of the specially pertinent volumes vary, but ordinarily mention "Census of Population" and "Characteristics of the Population."

California. Although Los Angeles began its spurt with the land boom of the 1880's, only with the 1920 census did its population surpass that of San Francisco. In the thirty years from 1920 to 1950, however, the southern city came to be almost three times as large as the northern. The 1950 census showed Los Angeles to rank as fourth largest in the nation, with just less than two million inhabitants. By 1952 it was officially estimated to have attained third rank by outgrowing Philadelphia. According to the 1950 census, the eight southernmost counties of California, which even with vast tracts of desert and mountains comprise only 29 per cent of the state's total area, have over 53 per cent of the total population. Entirely apart from the construction that chambers of commerce may place on these figures, they are obviously of great importance in dialect development.

The composition of California's population has been equally interesting. The proportion of foreign born has always been high, usually falling between 25 and 40 per cent of the total population, although there has been some slacking off in the last three decades. The city of San Francisco, for example, in 1870 had 49 per cent foreign-born population, and this proportion had dropped only to 22 per cent by 1940. Although roughly one-third to one-fourth of the foreign-born white population in California have usually come from English-speaking areas like the British Isles and Canada, there has always been a large segment of the citizenry whose mother tongue was not English. Among the most important foreign languages spoken in California have been Spanish, German, Italian, Chinese, Japanese, French, and Swedish.

In the nineteenth century, of Californians born in the United States but outside California itself, natives of New York state formed consistently the largest single element. By 1930 New Yorkers had dropped to fourth place behind natives of Illinois, Missouri, and Iowa. Natives of Illinois were not numerous in California before the turn of the century, but from 1910 to the present they have constituted the largest single element. Missourians have been second or third in frequency from the earliest settlement to the present. They ranked second to New Yorkers from 1850 to 1880, third to New Yorkers and Illinoisans from 1890 to 1910, and second to Illinoisans from 1920 to the present. New Englanders, notably those from Massachusetts and Maine, were an important element in California, especially in the San

Francisco Bay area, until about 1880. Natives of Pennsylvania and Ohio have come to California in significant numbers throughout the settlement period, but have never approached top rank in frequency. Since 1930 Oklahomans and Texans have migrated to California in large numbers and have presumably formed part of the great increase in Southern California population during recent years.

What dialect significance can the linguistic geographer find in these facts and figures of settlement history? First, it seems to me, he can recognize a number of factors in California favoring the establishment of language forms with widespread distributions in the East, and working against the more localized expressions from whatever Eastern area. The rapid growth of the population, its increased confinement to urban areas, the presence of large numbers of foreign language speakers who are dialectally neutral toward English, the relative heterogeneity of provenience of the native population with all Eastern areas except the deep South well represented—all these factors point to a dialect situation still largely in a state of flux, perhaps, but one in which forms in general use in the East stand the best chance of becoming established. Second, the dialectologist might assume from the settlement history that where a more local variant comes to prevail over the generally distributed Eastern word, it is likely to be of North Atlantic or North Central states origin, since natives of those areas have tended to predominate in all but the most recent periods of the state's settlement. Third, he might expect to find some dialect differentiation between Northern and Southern California, since their patterns of settlement by Easterners differ considerably.

It is not the point of this report to attempt to substantiate this third expectation, since in general the collection and analysis of data by the Linguistic Atlas of the Pacific Coast have not proceeded far enough to enable me to come to really valid conclusions on dialect differentiations within the state. I cannot resist, however, remarking on one clear Northern California dialect characteristic, which was discovered in our data more or less by accident. The word *chesterfield*, meaning "davenport, couch, or sofa," and found elsewhere on this continent principally in Canadian English, occurs in three-quarters of the questionnaires filled out in the area north of the ten southernmost counties of California and west of the Sierra Nevada. East of the Sierra in Northern California it

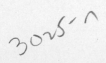

appears in only one-quarter of the individual responses, and in Southern California it is known to only one person in twenty. I suspect that it will be found west of the mountains in Washington and Oregon, but as yet have no proof of this.

The data to be presented here have a bearing on the first two matters mentioned above—the establishment in California of language forms with widespread distributions in the East, and the prevalence of an occasional more local variant at the expense of a more generally used Eastern term.

Following standard Linguistic Atlas procedures, the Atlas of the Pacific Coast began in 1949 to distribute vocabulary check lists in California and in 1952 to make field interviews. The California and Nevada section of the project calls for the collection by 1957 of 1,500 completed check lists and 300 interviews. At the present time about 600 check lists have been filled out and 85 interviews have been made. The material being reported on here is contained in the first 506 vocabulary check lists. Because the check lists are filled out directly by informants, usually without actual contact with an interviewer for the Linguistic Atlas, there are some difficulties in assessing their validity—the informant himself may not have all the requisite qualifications as to residence, age, and education; he may fill in what he thinks to be the "correct" word rather than the one he normally uses; or he may misinterpret the directions and mark only one word in each item rather than his full range of usage, as desired. Whatever flaws in validity may arise in occasional check lists, however, the large numbers of them that are filled out almost certainly give them greater reliability than the field interviews. Application of the statistical method of standard error[2] to the sample of 506 check lists now being reported on, reveals that the odds are 2 to 1 that the percentage frequencies found in the sample are within $2\frac{1}{4}$ per cent of the actual frequencies of usage in the population which the sample represents, and reveals further that the odds are 1000 to 1 that the sample frequencies are within $7\frac{1}{2}$ per cent of the actual frequencies of the whole population. It is expected that by the end of the project the comparison of highly valid data from field interviews with highly reliable data from vocabulary check

[2] See David W. Reed, "A Statistical Approach to Quantitative Linguistic Analysis," *Word*, V (1949), 235–247.

lists will make possible quite accurate statements about California dialect usage.

A word of caution should be given regarding the population represented by the sample of 506 check lists. This population is not the same as the population of California, in that the sample undoubtedly contains larger proportions of people from certain areas and with certain social characteristics than would be found in the total population of the state. For example, it is known that Northern California and rural California are more heavily represented than their share of the total population would warrant. Furthermore, the sample is unavoidably biased in representing only those people who are willing to take time to fill out a check list, and intentionally biased in including more long-time residents of single communities than one would find in the population as a whole. With these cautions in mind, it would be unwise to place too much reliance on the exact figures about to be presented, although they are certainly reliable enough to give a general indication of the fate of Eastern words in California.

The long table giving these percentages has been classified according to the Eastern distributions of the words in Kurath's *Word Geography of the Eastern United States*.[3] The first fourteen headings classify distributions in an order largely from the most general to the most localized. Localized words which, contrary to expectations, have prevailed in California over words of more general distribution appear separately in section 15, which also includes a few words that have come into much more general use in California than have most other words with similar Eastern distributions. In sub-classifying the words and expressions in category 15, I have also indicated their distribution in the Great Lakes region, according to A. L. Davis's *Word Atlas of the Great Lakes Region*,[4] since the behavior of a dialect term in the North Central states often foreshadows its fate in California.

Proceeding to a detailed consideration of the table, we note that words in sections 1 and 2, those of general and almost general distribution in the East, have tended to become majority usage in California. Exceptions to this rule are explained partially by

[3] Ann Arbor: University of Michigan Press, 1949. I have not thought it necessary to cite page references for the discussion of each individual dialect term in Kurath, since the book is carefully indexed.

[4] Microfilm diss. Ann Arbor: University of Michigan, 1949.

the cross references to competing words in section 15. *Barnyard*, for example, is no more frequent than 53 per cent, because of the competition of the Western word *corral* (section 15.4) which occurs in 51 per cent of the check lists. Use of the general word *bread* to refer to a loaf made with white flour appears in a deceptively low 44 per cent of the check lists, largely because the expanded form *white bread* also appears in 44 per cent of the questionnaires. Kurath reports principally three expanded forms in the East: *white bread* in Eastern New England, *wheat bread* in the remainder of the North and North Midlands, and *light bread* in the South and South Midlands. Davis reports *wheat bread* no further west than Ohio, and gives *white bread* and *light bread* as the usual Northern and Midland expanded forms respectively in the Great Lakes region. If *wheat bread* was ever common in California, it has apparently died out because of confusion with *wheat bread* as an abbreviated form of *wholewheat bread*. There is no actual conflict between *bread* and *white bread* in California usage. *White bread* is merely the normal expanded form of the general word.

Seesaw is used in California only to about the same extent as *teeter-totter* (15.2) in spite of a more general distribution in the Atlantic coast states. The generally distributed *pancake* is a poor second to *hot cake*, unfortunately not included in Davis's study, but limited according to Kurath to eastern Pennsylvania. The limited use of *hot cake* as a folk term in the East may obscure a fact of general use in formal English. In parts of the Middle West where I have lived, one is likely to make *pancakes* at home, but to order *hot cakes* in a restaurant. It would seem much more likely that California preference for the term *hot cake* derives from formal usage rather than from the popular speech of eastern Pennsylvania. Another Western word, *flapjack* (15.4), occurs with a frequency of 7 per cent. It seems to be limited in application to a pancake made over a campfire rather than in a kitchen.

(Sick) at his stomach, the general Eastern expression, is slightly less frequent than *to his stomach* (15.1), a phrase limited to the Northern dialect in the Atlantic coast and Great Lakes states. *Lightning bug*, the general Eastern term, is considerably less frequent than *firefly* (15.2), a Northern term on the Atlantic coast, which becomes distributed more generally in the Great Lakes region. This development may be due in part to the fact that there are no lightning bugs in California. Confusion as to the

nature of the beast is apparent in section 15.5 with the occurrence of *glow worm* in this meaning at a frequency of 11 per cent.

Burlap (*bag* or *sack*), terms of almost general distribution in the East, fare badly in competition with *gunny* (*sack* or *bag*) (15.2), terms which first appear in the upper Ohio valley, but become general in the Great Lakes region. There may be in the prevalence of *gunny sack* a reflection of the fact that California's rural population, which has primarily to deal with the article, derives more from the North Central than the North Atlantic states. A Western expression, *barley sack* (15.4), also occurs with this meaning in 6 per cent of the check lists. Finally, in section 2, the almost general Eastern expression, *a bite* (*to eat*), fares badly in competition with the equally general *snack*. The development of *snack bars* may have had something to do with the favoring of the latter.

Looking next at sections 3, 5, and 7, we observe that expressions occurring throughout two of the three major speech areas tend to predominate in California usage if not in competition with even more generally distributed Eastern terms. Exceptions to this rule are *clingstone* (*peach*) (3), *baby carriage* (5), and *comfort* (7). The competitors of the first two, *cling* (*peach*) (15.3) and *baby buggy* (15.2) begin as Western Pennsylvania words and hold their own or become more general in the Great Lakes region. The rival that is displacing the third in California, *comforter* (15.1), is an exclusively Northern term in the Atlantic coast and Great Lakes states. It may have become so general in California as a result of mail-order catalogue usage. The occurrence in section 15.5 of the term *quilt* with this same meaning in 35 per cent of the check lists reveals a confusion on the item, since it was described in the question as "tied *not* quilted."

Turning now to sections 4.1 and 6.1, we note that words used throughout the North and in any additional area tend to predominate in California usage if not in competition with more generally distributed terms. The only clear exception is (*hay*) *cock* (4.1), which finishes a poor second to (*hay*) *shock* (15.3), the Southernmost of the terms which occur with unexpected frequency in California. One may perhaps question whether the popularity of (*hay*) *shock* has not been considerably promoted by a euphemistic disfavoring of (*hay*) *cock*.

In the remaining sections of the table, except 15—that is 4.2, 6.2, and 8 through 14—we observe that words which occur in restricted parts of two major dialect areas or wholly within one major dialect area tend to be in minority usage or nonexistent in California. Most of the words in section 15 are exceptions to this rule, and in addition we may note *clabber(ed)* (*milk*) (8.1), a term in use everywhere south of the Mason-Dixon Line, which seems to predominate in California largely because most of its Eastern rivals are of extremely localized occurrence. In fact, its principal competitor is *sour(ed) milk* (15.5), an expression which I ascribe to the lack of need for discrimination of the varying degrees of sourness in the typical urban environment.

The sub-classification of words in section 15 demonstrates that most of the terms which have attained to frequent use in California in the face of competition from more generally distributed words in the Atlantic coast states, are Northern, Midland, or both. They are, moreover, all words of fairly general distribution in the Great Lakes region. *Chivaree* (15.2) has, after a nationwide study,[5] been found to occur throughout the area of French settlement of the United States and everywhere west of that settlement area.

In section 15.4 the only Western word that has not already come up for discussion is *grate*, which occurs in 20 per cent of the check lists as an alternate or substitute for *andirons*. The device in a California fireplace often consists of both two large supports for logs and a metal basket for paper, kindling, or coal. In this case *andirons* or *grate* is applied indiscriminately to the entire device, and the original distinction is forgotten.

While some of the terms in section 15.5—*eaves* and *drainpipes* meaning *gutters* or *eaves troughs*, *breastbone* meaning *wishbone* or *pulley bone*, *worm* meaning *angleworm* or *fish(ing) worm*, and *haystack* meaning *hay shock* or *hay cock*—may ultimately prove characteristic of California folk speech, the best guess at present is that their frequency is due largely to urban unfamiliarity with the item in question.

In rapid final summary, the popularity of a word in California tends to reflect the generality of its distribution in Eastern dialects. Words that occur everywhere in the East or in parts of the three major dialect areas or throughout two major dialect areas or throughout the North and in parts of another area, usually predominate in California. Words that occur in parts of two major

[5] A. L. Davis and R. I. McDavid, "*Shivaree*: An Example of Cultural Diffusion," *American Speech*, XXIV (1949), 249–255.

areas or exclusively in a single major area tend to be in minority usage or nonexistent in California. Words which in spite of this last kind of distribution in the East are unexpectedly frequent in California are usually Northern, Midland, or partly both in the Atlantic coast states and at least moderately frequent in the Great Lakes region. It is hoped that more detailed analysis of the California materials, including especially the field interviews, will reveal other dialect lines within the state like that noted in the case of the word *chesterfield*.

TABLE

PERCENTAGE FREQUENCY OF EASTERN WORDS IN CALIFORNIA CHECK LISTS

1. Words of general distribution, Atlantic coast states.

Merry Christmas	99	to shell	72
(clothes) closet	98	hauling	69
faucet	96	andirons	68
(just) a (little) way(s)	95	dragon fly	61
hay stack	94	moo	59
picket fence	92	barnyard [cf. 15.4]	53
corn bread	92	bread [cf. 15.1]	44
midwife	90	seesaw [cf. 15.2]	44
wishbone	81	pancake [cf. 15.3]	43
cottage cheese	79	at his stomach [cf. 15.1]	41
frying pan	72	lightning bug [cf. 15.2]	29

2. Words occurring in parts of North, Midlands, and South (almost general).

(window) shades	86	(Hudson Valley, South, and urban)
(hay or barn) loft	81	(North, South Midlands, South)
string beans	80	(North, Eastern Penna., Chesapeake Bay)
(wooden or well) bucket	76	(Eastern New England, Midlands, South)
a snack	63	(South, South Midlands, and urban)
gutters	46	(E. New England, New York City, E. Pa., South)
so (boss) (ie)	42	(General exc. Virginia)
burlap (bag or sack) [cf. 15.2]	26	(North, North Midlands, Virginia)
a bite [see *snack* above]	16	(New England, Hudson Valley, E. Pa., Ches. Bay)

3. Words occurring throughout the North and Midlands.

clingstone (peach) [cf. 15.3]	50	clothes press [cf. 1]	0

4. Words occurring in parts of the North and Midlands.
   4.1 Throughout the North and North Midlands

skunk	93	(hay) mow [cf. 2]	21
(corn) husks	81	(hay) cock [cf. 15.3]	18
whinny	43	wheat bread [cf. 1 and 15.1]	3
quarter of [cf. 5]	27		

   4.2 Parts of New England and Midlands

fish worm [cf. 15.1]	21	(New England, Hudson Val., E. Pa., West Va.)
heap (of hay) [cf. 4.1, 15.3]	0	(Eastern New England and Pennsylvania)
bonny clabber [cf. 8.1]	0	(Eastern New England and E. Pennsylvania)

5. Words occurring throughout the North and South.

quarter to	66	(wooden) pail [cf. 2]	18
baby carriage [cf. 15.2]	23		

6. Words occurring in parts of the North and South.
   6.1 Throughout the North and part of the South

kerosene	64	(Carolinas)
curtains [cf. 2, 11]	5	(Virginia and Coastal North Carolina)

   6.2 Parts of New England and the South

low [cf. 1]	11	(South and scattered in New England)
serenade [cf. 15.2]	11	(E. New England and South, scat. elsewhere)
yeast bread [cf. 1, 15.1]	3	(E. New England and Chesapeake Bay)
lucky bone [cf. 1]	0	(NE. New England and Virginia)
whicker [cf. 4.1, 8.2]	0	(E. New England and South exc. Virginia)

7. Words occurring throughout the Midlands and South.

(milk or water) bucket	75	pulley bone [cf. 1]	4
coal oil [M. & Ches. B.]	53	spicket [cf. 1]	2
skillet [cf. 1]	34	paling fence [cf. 1]	2
comfort [cf. 15.1]	21	corn pone [cf. 1]	2
saw (boss) [cf. 2]	12		

8. Words occurring in parts of the Midlands and South.
   8.1 Everywhere south of the Mason-Dixon Line

clabber(ed) (milk)	57	barn lot [exc. Md.; cf. 1, 15.4]	2
(corn) shucks [cf. 4.1]	17	dog irons [exc. Md.; cf. 1]	2

light bread [cf. 1, 15.1]   16   granny [also W. Pa.; cf. 1]   1
Christmas Gift! [cf. 1]   3   fire dogs [cf. 1]   0

8.2 Virginia and West Midland
nicker [cf. 4.1]   26   lamp oil [cf. 6.1, 7]   2
snake doctor [cf. 1]   9   plum peach [cf. 3, 15.3]   0
fishing worm [cf. 15.1]   4

8.3 Restricted parts of the Midlands and South
smearcase [cf. 1]   12   (North Midland and Chesapeake
                                         Bay)
in his stomach [cf. 1, 15.1]   11   (S. Penna., Chesapeake Bay, Coastal
                                         N. Car.)
pile (of hay) [cf. 4.1, 15.3]   8   (E. Pennsylvania and South)
quarter till [cf. 4.1, 5]   4   (West Midland and North Carolina)
a (little) piece [cf. 1]   4   (Midland and North Carolina)
(hay) rick [cf. 1]   2   (E. Pennsylvania and Virginia)
granny woman [cf. 1]   0   (West Virginia, Ches. Bay, and N.
                                         Car.)

9. Words occurring throughout the North.
   (milk or water) pail [cf. 7] 34   johnny cake [cf. 1]   7
   eaves troughs (cf. 2)   18   spider [cf. 1]   4
   darning needle [cf. 1]   13

10. Words occurring in part of the North.
    10.1 Throughout New England and in some other Northern area
    teeter(ing) (board) [cf. 1,
       15.2]   26   (New York)
    Dutch cheese [cf. 1]   6   (All of North but the Hudson Valley)
    loo [cf. 1]   4   (New York)
    carting [cf. 1]   2   (New York, New Jersey)
    drawing [cf. 1]   0   (Hudson Valley)

    10.2 Restricted parts of the North
    eaves spouts [cf. 2]   1   (Northern New England and Western
                                          Reserve)
    lobbered milk [cf. 8.1]   0   (Western New England and New
                                          York)
    comfortable [cf. 7, 15.1]   0   (SW. New England and Hudson
                                          Valley)
    raised bread [cf. 1, 15.1]   0   (Eastern New England)
    teaming [cf. 1]   0   (Eastern Massachusetts)
    fritter [cf. 1, 15.3]   0   (Northeastern New England)
    cow yard [cf. 1, 15.4]   0   (Eastern New England)
    ground mow [cf. 2]   0   (Eastern New England)
    high beams (cf. 2)   0   (Northeastern New England)
    (hay) tumble [cf. 4.1, 15.3] 0   (Northeastern New England)

great beams [cf. 2]   0   (Central Massachusetts)
Dutch cap [cf. 4.1, 15.3]   0   (Southeastern New England)
pot cheese (cf. 1]   0   (Hudson Valley)
(hay) barrack [cf. 1]   0   (Hudson Valley)

11. Words occurring throughout the Midlands.
(window) blinds [cf. 2]   27   spouts, spouting [cf. 2]   1
to hull [cf. 1]   13   spigot [cf. 1]   1
snake feeder [cf. 1]   6

12. Words occurring in part of the Midlands.
green beans [cf. 2]   17   (Western Pennsylvania and South
                                  Midlands)
fire bug [cf. 1, 15.2]   7   (Pennsylvania)
piece [food] [cf. 2]   6   (Pennsylvania)
cruddled milk [cf. 8.1]   3   (Pennsylvania)
hand stack [cf. 4.1, 15.3]   3   (Pennsylvania)
thick milk [cf. 8.1]   2   (Pennsylvania)
overhead, overden [cf. 2]   0   (Pennsylvania)
paled fence [cf. 1]   0   (Eastern Pennsylvania)
(hay) doodle (cf. 4.1, 15.3] 0   (Western Pennsylvania and Ohio
                                  Valley)
carbon oil [cf. 6.1, 7]   0   (Western Pennsylvania)
hap [cf. 7, 15.1]   0   (Western Pennsylvania)

13. Words occurring throughout the South.
carrying [cf. 1]   29   batter cakes [cf. 1, 15.3]   0
snap beans [cf. 2]   4

14. Words occurring in part of the South.
mosquito hawk [cf. 1]   9   (South except Virginia)
earthworm [cf. 15.1]   8   (North Carolina, learned elsewhere)
hand irons [cf. 1]   2   (Chesapeake Bay)
tow sack [cf. 2, 15.2]   1   (North Carolina)
guano sack [cf. 2, 15.2]   0   (Virginia and Maryland)
croker sack [cf. 2, 15.2]   0   (Virginia and South Carolina)
press peach [cf. 3, 15.3]   0   (South except Virginia)
(sea) grass sack [cf. 2, 15.2] 0 (Chesapeake Bay)
pale yard [cf. 1]   0   (North Carolina)
walling [cf. 1]   0   (Eastern North Carolina)

15. Words of "unexpected" frequency.
15.1 Primarily Northern
comforter   94   (New England, New York, Northern
                                  Great Lakes)
angleworm   53   (Northern, including Northern Great
                                  Lakes)

to his stomach   46   (Northern, including Northern Great Lakes)

white bread   44   (Eastern New England, Michigan, Ohio)

15.2 North and Midland

baby buggy   85   (Western Pennsylvania, Ohio Valley, Great Lakes)

chivaree   78   (Northern New England, S. Midland, Gt. Lakes exc. Ohio)

gunny (sack or bag)   66   (Ohio Valley, Great Lakes)

firefly   54   (New England, New York, Penna., Great Lakes)

teeter totter   43   (New York, New Jersey, Great Lakes)

15.3 Primarily Midland

hot cakes   65   (Eastern Penna. [no inform. from Great Lakes])

cling (peach)   55   (Western Penna., South Midland, Midland Gt. Lakes)

(hay) shocks   55   (South of Mason-Dixon, Midland Great Lakes)

15.4 Western

corral   51

grate   20

flapjacks   7

barley sack   6

15.5 Due to urban unfamiliarity with item?

sour(ed) milk	46	breast bone	19
quilt	35	worm	19
eaves	21	hay stack [meaning *shock*]	12
drain pipes	20	glow worm	11

SUPPLEMENTARY LIST OF SOUTH CAROLINA WORDS AND PHRASES

F. W. BRADLEY

University of South Carolina

INTRODUCTION

Since this is a follow-up of a list of words in *PADS*, No. 14 (November, 1950), the opportunity is offered to make some corrections. On pages 17 and 41 of that list, the *bullfinch* and *joree* are defined erroneously as the *green-tailed towhee*. This should be the *red-eyed towhee*. Mr. W. L. McAtee kindly called attention to these errors.

The word *colcock*, rather widely used in South Carolina, meaning to knock out, to knock unconscious, is not dialectal, but gangster slang. It is probably derived from the name of a type of blackjack consisting of a leathern pouch, five or six inches long, filled with shot and used by gangsters to blackjack their victims. Its resemblance to *membrum virile flaccidum* would give rise to the name. In the *American Thesaurus of Slang*, cold-cock is defined either as a knock-out blow, or, as a verb, to knock out. But in spite of the fact that *cold cock* has not as yet been found in the sense of a blackjack, I am persuaded that this is the origin of the slang word. This theory was suggested to me by one of our correspondents.

The word *snollygoster*, ascribed to the South, but heard only rarely in this State, recently attracted considerable attention because of its use in high political circles. An editorial in the *Courier Express* of Buffalo says that the word means a political job seeker, a fellow who wants office regardless of party, platform or principles, and ends by saying that he achieves his purpose by the sheer force of "monumental talknophical assumnacy," This is quoted from the *Dictionary of Americanisms*, which defines the word as a pretentious boaster. I offer the following observations as a possible solution for the origin of this word.[1]

[1] [According to a U.P. item from New York, with dateline of November 11, 1953, former President Truman commented that his Republican critics were "snollygosters," going on to say, "In case you're wondering about that word 'snollygoster,' it's a Southern word meaning a man born out of wedlock." Another U.P. item from Atlanta of the same date states that "the man who coined the word was the late Col. H. W. J. Hamm, once editor of

16

The *English Dialect Dictionary* lists *snoll*, a variant of *snool*, ⌐
a verb meaning to slobber, to dribble. *Snooling* is given as an adjective of contempt. This dictionary also gives the word *gauster*, which as a verb means to bully, bluster, storm, be turbulent, boisterous, brag, boast, swagger. As a noun it means swagger, brag, idle talk, gossip, nonsense; applied to a person it means a violent and unmanageable fellow, a swaggerer, a fool. I offer the explanation of this word as being a compound of *snoll* and *gauster* after the analogy of words like *slapdash*, *slambang*, since the meanings of both *snoll* and *gauster* are borne by this word *snollygoster*. I should not be at all surprised if it is known pretty generally outside the South. It is true that *snoll* and *gauster* are from the *English Dialect Dictionary* and not from an American reference work, but the *Dictionary of Americanisms* cites from the West the word *gostration*, which is the act of putting on airs, and which is probably related to the word *gauster*.

The dialectal pronunciation of *drain* as *dreen* is widespread and common throughout the northwestern half of South Carolina. A section of the Dutch Fork lying between Wateree Creek and the town of Chapin also uses [-in] in other words which in standard speech have [-en], so that *crane* is pronounced *creen*; *grain*, *green*; *pane*, *peen*; *rain*, *reen*; *train*, *treen*, etc. In the same neighborhood occur the pronunciations *boon*, *droon*, *groon*, *stoon*, etc. for *bone*, *drone*, *groan*, *stone*, etc. If these peculiarities appear in any other regions in the state they have not been reported.

In Williamsburg County there is a pure compensatory lengthening for the disappearance of the *r* in pronunciation: bird [bɜːd], third [θɜːd], heard [hɜːd]. I do not know how widespread this is; I have heard it only from that county. What one regularly hears is [bɜɪd], etc.

Probably a result of careless speech not confined to any region are such pronunciations as *hank you* for "thank you" and *I hink*

---

the old Georgia Cracker newspaper in Gainesville, Georgia, now the Gainesville News. Hamm thought it up in a speech about 60 years ago." Inasmuch as the first quotation in DA is dated 1862, this etymology is as incredible as Mr. Truman's definition. In western Maryland, a snollygoster (more usually *snallygaster*) is a mythical bird. One terrorized the Middletown Valley a number of years ago. It got an excellent press, particularly in the Baltimore Sunpapers. See also Leo Spitzer, "A Futher Note on 'Snollygoster'," *American Speech*, XXIX (1954), 85.—Ed.]

so for "I think so." People who do this are apparently unconscious of it and would probably deny doing so. Careless speech may also be responsible for a treatment of *doesn't, hasn't isn't, wasn't*, which become respectively [dʌdn̩], [hædn̩], [ɪdn̩], [wʌdn̩]. "I am going to...." has become step by step: [aɪm gonə], [aɪ monə], [aɪmõ, aɪmo]. Such departures from standard speech are probably more or less general in the South.

The method followed in assembling this collection of folk speech is the same as that described in *PADS*, No. 14. Correspondents were stimulated through a long series of articles appearing in all the Sunday newspapers to send in words and phrases which they considered peculiar. Discussion of these words and phrases formed a large part of the newspaper articles. When these efforts seemed to have reached the point of diminishing returns, a list was sifted out of the correspondence and mimeographed. This list was then mailed out to about thirty correspondents in various sections for their comments.

Correspondents indicated whether or not they knew the various words in their locality; thus, the distribution of a usage was determined. Evidently these results can be only approximately true to the facts. A word may not have been heard by a correspondent, and yet be in daily use in restricted circles.

Correspondents who have contributed most to this list are: Miss Rose Aldrich, Miss Anna Blake, Professor Norman Chamberlain, Dr. Hennig Cohen, Mr. Richard G. Coker, Miss Laura De Shields, Mrs. J. L. Drafts, Mrs. L. J. DuBose, Professor Chlo Fink, Dr. T. A. FitzGerald, Miss Kathleen Fogartie, Dr. R. B. Furman, Mrs. Arthur Gaillard, Mr. R. T. Griggs, Professor H. H. Jenkins, Mr. C. M. McKinnon, Mrs. Laura Miles, Dr. Chapman Milling, Miss Louise Pettus, Colonel F. G. Potts, Mrs. T. A. Price, Mr. Olin J. Salley, Dr. M. B. Seigler, Mr. Samuel G. Stoney, Mrs. Jane P. Strother, Mr. C. W. Stuckey, Dr. G. W. Walker, Dr. J. E. Whitesell, Dr. Celesta Wine, Dr. H. J. Woods. Most of these have also checked the list for further suggestions. There are, however, many scores of other people to whom thanks are due for contributions and suggestions.

ABBREVIATIONS:

ATS: L. V. Berrey and M. Van den Bark, *American Thesaurus of Slang*, New York, 1952.

DA: M. M. Mathews, *Dictionary of Americanisms*, Chicago, 1951.

EDD: Joseph Wright, *English Dialect Dictionary*, London, 1898–1905.

G.P.W.: George P. Wilson, "Folk Speech" in the *Frank C. Brown Collection of North Carolina Folklore*, Durham, N. C., 1952, I, 503–618.

Wen.: Harold Wentworth, *American Dialect Dictionary*, New York, 1944.

WNID: *Webster's New International Dictionary*, Springfield Mass., 1950.

GLOSSARY

absquatulize: *v.i.* "To top one's broom, to hop the twig, to go on leg bail" (Camden [S.C.] *Journal*, July 3, 1829, p. 3, column 2). "To hop the twig" and "to top one's broom" are apparently both as obsolete as *absquatulize*. DA, *absquatalize*.

again: *adv.* Hereafter, from now on; at all. There is no idea of repetition implied. "John is fifty and still a bachelor. Do you think he will ever marry?" "No, not *again*." "If you haven't sent that letter, I wouldn't send it *again*." "I've changed my mind about that trip. It's too expensive. I won't go *again*." "If he hasn't come by now, he certainly will not come *again*." I have been assured that this peculiar usage is widely heard outside of South Carolina, but do not find it listed. Cf. EDD, *again*, B. adv. 1, at a future time, by-and-by. "When will yah come then?" "Oh, *again*." (I.e., not now, next time.)

all-day singing: *n.* An all-day religious songfest with picnic lunch on the grounds. Georgia. Probably northwest South Carolina also, but not so reported. *All-day singing* is a custom of long standing, according to reliable reports. The songs are hymns or spiritual songs sung by all, but varied often with quartets or choruses. The tone is one of happiness, joy, and relaxation, and good performance of quartets is greeted with hearty applause. Basket lunches provide the midday meal. An *all-night singing* was recently reported from Florida, in the Tampa *Morning Tribune*, July 12, 1953.

all over: *adv.* Everywhere. *Anywhere, somewhere, everywhere* are all being crowded out of popular speech by *any place, some place, every place*, or *all over*. I recall hearing *any place* in the sense of "anywhere" in 1898 on a phonograph record with "an original

Yankee story" by Cal Stewart. It was at that time entirely un-
known here, I believe.

allust: *adv.* Always. Wen. *allus.* Lancaster County. (Excrescent
t.)

antigodlin: *adj.* Same as *squawed, q.v.* Wen.

Ash Nanny: *n.* Biscuit dough cooked on a board before the open
fire.

Aunt Hagar's chillun, Hagar's chillun: *n. pl.* A phrase used by
Negroes to designate themselves. Not frequently heard.

ball: *n.* One of the two bulging sides of a bale of cotton, i.e., the
two sides which were subjected to pressure in baling.

banty chicken: *n.* A bantam. Also called *banty.* EDD, *banty.*
[*Banty chicken* and *banty* are both current in Western Maryland.—
Ed.]

barefoot: *adj.* Straight, unmixed, as to take one's coffee *barefoot.*
John's Island.

bellowsed: *past part., adj.* Affected with the heaves, said of a
horse. EDD, *bellows, v.,* to breathe hard.

billdaget ['bil₁dægɪt]: *n.* A wooden pestle formerly used to pound
rice in a wooden mortar, to separate the grains from the husk.
Probably such a pestle is still so used, but the word is not reported
in current use. This seems to be a variant of *gillgadget (q.v.)*, by
faulty hearing or otherwise. See also *gillhicket,* below. George-
town and Charleston area.

blab-mouth: *n.* One who blabs, chatters, gossips; *blab-mouthed,*
adj. (*Blabber-mouthed* as an adjective was used by Mr. Elmer
Davis in a daily newscast on December 3, 1952.) EDD, *blab-mouth.*

Black Border: *n.* The coastal region of South Carolina, with its
predominance of Negro population. Title of a collection of Gullah
stories by Ambrose Gonzales.

blazed: *past part., adj.* Blaze-faced. Cf. WNID, *blaze, n.* Lancaster County.

bless out: *v.t.* To scold, to revile. Not necessarily and not usually
to curse. Cf. WNID, *bless,* v.t., 8.

block and tickle: *n.* Block and tackle. *DN,* I, 211 gives *block and
takle. PADS,* No. 11, p. 12.

bloodymenoun ['blʌdɪmɪ'naʊn]: *n.* A bullfrog. Cf. *PADS,* No.
14, p. 15, *blood and 'ounds.* Sumter County, Pee Dee and Eastern
section.

blow one's bone : *v. phr.* To drool as an infant beginning to teethe. "Dat chile *blowin' 'e bone.*" Gullah.

book [bʊk]: *v.i.* and *v.t.* To push with the horns; to hook. "Look out, that cow *books.* She will *book* you." EDD., Wen. give *buck* in a similar sense.

boomalally [ˈbʊməˌlælɪ]: *n.* "Formerly (down to 1900) applied only to a cadet of the South Carolina Military Academy" (John Bennett, of Charleston, S.C., also others from Charleston area). Later applied to any soldier, especially to one on parade marching to music. The name seems to be derived from the sound of the drum.[2] Charleston.

boon, droon, groon, stoon, etc. for *bone, drone, groan, stone, etc.*: See Introduction.

bootleg : *n.* See under *shirtsleeve.*

bouk [bʊk]: *n.* The psalterium. WNID gives the pronunciation [buk], but this pronunciation has never been reported in S.C. The word is widely known and used by butchers and by farmers who slaughter their own cattle. I recall from childhood supposing that it was called "book" because it had so many "leaves" in it. EDD, with pronunciation not indicated.

brown jug : *n.* A biscuit with a hole punched into it with the forefinger and filled with molasses. Also called a *molasses jug.* Sumter and Darlington Counties. *Molasses biscuit* (see *PADS*, No. 14, p. 47) is more generally used. Mainly used by children.

brush broom, bresh broom, yard broom : *n.* A broom made by binding small branches together for sweeping the yard. Dogwood branches are preferred for their toughness. Gallberry is also used. Wen. lists *brushbroom (bresh-broom),* but does not define. Cf. *stumpy broom.*

brush harbor : *n.* An arbor formed by stringing wire or poles on the top of posts, over which leafy branches are laid to form a dense shade for the comfort of people attending a camp meeting for religious

[2] *Boomalally* is also used in refrains and yells:

"Boomalally, boomalally, bow, wow, wow,
Chickalally, chickalally, chow, chow, chow:
Boomalally, chickalally, who are we?
We are the boys of ——— C. [College]."

When I first received a report on this word, it sounded a bit fantastic, but I soon found that anyone who had lived in Charleston forty years ago was familiar with it.

worship. Often seen by the roadside in summer. See Wen. under *redundant h*. DA, illustrated under *brush arbor*.

buggy: *v.i.* To go away, to leave. Cf. *haul buggy*. Dutch Fork.

build: *v.t.* To make. Reported only concerning the making of coffee in an urn. Neologism. Columbia.

bull-footed: *adj*. Awkward, clumsy. This may be reminiscent of the proverbial phrase, "A bull in a china shop." Also *bumble-footed*.

bump: *v.t.* A form of hazing among school boys in which the victim is swung face upward by two boys, one on each side, who hold one foot and one hand each. The victim is then swung backward and forward against a tree so that his rump strikes the tree. Sometimes two victims are bumped against each other instead of against a tree. EDD, *bump*. This form of hazing was formerly practiced in the Dutch Fork on the careless harvesting hand who failed to glean all the heads of grain. *Buck*, *v.t.* is reported with this meaning in *DN*, I, 63 and II, 24.

bunglesome, bungersome: *adj*. Of awkward, clumsy shape for handling, applied to packages, bundles, etc. Not applied to persons, so far as reported. WNID, *bunglesome*, dial. Wen. *bungersome*, clumsy. Cf. EDD, *bunglesome, adj.*, muddled, tangled, confused.

bush: *v.t.* To *bush* a building is to fasten a green *bush* to the topmost part of the framework when the frame is completed. The custom is doubtless imported from Europe, where it still is observed. See the *National Geographic Magazine*, August, 1950, p. 219. It has been reported from Charleston during the last decade. It was also observed in Hartsville in 1926 when the pulp plant of the Sonoco Products Company was constructed. Correspondents from the Middle West write that this custom was once observed there, but not during the last thirty years. It has also been reported to me verbally from Mexico and from New York City.[3]

bush: *n*. The *bush* referred to under *bush, v.t.*

bush chillun: See *woods chillun*.

butler's polish: *n*. A phrase denoting perfection, in the phrase "to a butler's polish," i.e., to perfection. "He has done this job to a *butler's polish*."

---

[3] The bush was usually a small tree, and the fact that the occasion called for some show of largesse on the part of the builder gave rise to the common expression "A tree, a treat." The treat is reported to have been a keg of beer, a picnic, or a gift of groceries to the workmen.

buttbroke: *past part.*, *adj.* Of a cloak having the rear lines spoiled by bagging, caused by wearing the cloak while sitting. Cf. *rump-sprung.*

buzzard lope: *n.* A dancing step, apparently in imitation of the hopping of a buzzard as it is about to rise in flight, or when hopping around a carcass. General. DA.

by sun: *phr.* The time before sundown is measured, as two hours *by sun*, a half hour *by sun*, etc.

care [kjɛə]: *v.t.* and *v.i.* This pronunciation is fairly general, even among educated people.

carry: *n.* The amount of meat, especially numbles, given to each person engaged in hog killing, to be taken home. Also called *totin's.* Sometimes applied also to what the cook takes home daily. Charleston and environs. ?Obsolescent.

carry straws: *v. phr.* To go courting. "He is *carrying straws* for Mary." This is taken from the habits of the male bird in the mating season. Lexington County.

case dollar: *n.* A whole dollar, not a dollar in change. Some take this to mean a silver dollar. Cf. DA, *case dollar.*

ceasted: *past tense* and *past part.* Deceased. Negro usage.

chaney briar: *n.* See *wild asparagus.*

chap: *n.* A small boy. Not often used for adults, except by people who have come into the State from the outside. In the plural: children, boys and girls. *Girl chap* as reported by Wen. is not heard here. Teen-age girls are called chaps in the Dutch Fork. The usual expression is *gal baby* (not necessarily an infant) or sometimes *girl baby.* Cf. DA.

chaw: *v.t.* To chew. Besides the usual nonstandard use, *chaw* is used in the following sentence: I don't *chaw* my tobacco ('backer) but once. Sometimes is added "and I spit where I please." This is an intentionally offensive and challenging refusal to repeat one's words. A more polite refusal is "Shakespeare never repeats." *Chaw* is not usually felt to be slang; it is a widespread nonstandard variant of *chew.* Cf. DA, *chaw*, EDD, *chaw.*

China grass: *n.* See *sapphire grass.*

chop out: *v.t.* To thin out the stand of cotton with a hoe. Also simply *to chop.* Wen. gives the verb *chop* with the meaning "to hoe." In South Carolina the cotton is first *chopped out*, and later hoed to remove crabgrass from between the growing stalks. A crop may be hoed several times, according to need. *Chop* and *hoe* are thus not synonymous.

chowder: *n*. The entire cornstalk, ears, and shucks ground for cattle feed. Timmonsville.

chuffy: *adj*. Surly. Same as WNID, *chuff*, ill-tempered; sulky, surly, cross. Obs. exc. dial.

clear seed: *adj*. Freestone as applied to peaches. Also *free seed*, *open stone*.

clew: *v.t., past tense* and *past part., clewed, clewted*. To strike a person, usually on the head with the fist. Cf. EDD, *clew, sb*. 2. Chesterfield County.

clove: *past tense* of *cleave*, to stick, to adhere. WNID notes this as archaic.

couch [kutʃ]: *v.t*. To transfer a layer of pulp from the wire screen to the felt, in paper manufacturing. *Couch roll* is also used as a noun. EDD gives our pronunciation as a variant. Cf. WNID *couch, v.t*. 2. Hartsville. May be general in paper manufacturing.

courting scarf: *n*. A rectangular scarf long enough to go over the shoulders of two people together.

cracked cotton: *n*. Cotton bolls that are only slightly open. Wen., *crack*, to open slightly. Lancaster County.

crawl: *v.i*. To creep on all fours, as of an infant. [Infants crawl] in Maryland, too.—Ed.] Also in the phrases "to make the flesh *crawl*" and "to make the stomach *crawl*."

creassy greens: *n.pl*. Watercress. Reported sporadically from Sumter and the northwestern sections. Cf. Zeta C. Davison, "A Word-List from the Appalachians and the Piedmont Area of North Carolina," *PADS*, No. 19, p. 10, *creasy-greens*.

cried: *past part*. Announced. Only in the phrase "to be cried in meeting," i.e., to have one's engagement announced in church. Wen.; WNID, *cry, v.t*. 3, b.

cush [kuʃ]: *n*. In coastal S.C., corn meal mixed with water, cooked in bacon grease. In the upcountry, corn bread mashed up in bacon grease to a homogeneous mass. In the central section, fried scrapple is called cush, also corn meal fried with meat or oysters. Always a mixture is involved. [Cf. *PADS*, No. 11, p. 5. *Dictionary of American English*, DA, WNID. As M. M. Mathews has pointed out, using the researches of Lorenzo D. Turner as his source, the word is an Africanism (originally Arabic) of Gullah transmission (*Some Sources of Southernisms*, University, Ala., 1948, pp. 120–

124). Turner lists the word in his *Africanisms in the Gullah Dialect* (Chicago, 1949), p. 197.—Ed.]

cymling, simling, simlin: *n.* A variety of dwarf watermelon found in cotton fields. It seldom grows bigger than the double fist, with seeds correspondingly small. The flesh is of a yellowish or pale pink color and far inferior in taste to the watermelon. Dutch Fork, Abbeville, Greenwood, McCormick Counties and sporadically in the coastal area. [In the sense "squash," *simlin* is Standard English.—Ed.]

cymling-head: *n.* A silly person; a dolt. Lexington County. Wen., **cymblin-head.**

daffydil: *n.* Any flower of the narcissus, jonquil or daffodil family. Charleston, among colored girls selling flowers, also in northeast and northwest sections.

devil dancing: *n.* Dancing in which the feet may be crossed; dancing as an expression of animal spirits. Holy dancing, in religious services, is a sort of lively rhythmic shuffle with many worshipers taking part. It is an expression of religious emotion, in which the feet are never crossed. The participants are those who have had the experience of conversion, and the dance is an expression of happiness over the event. Rather general among Negroes. Cf. DA, *devil-dance.*

devil's riding horse: *n.* The praying mantis. Also Johnny cock-horse, devil's horse.

devil's walking stick: *n.* A stick insect, the *diapheromera femorata.* WNID, *walking stick,* b.

dew poison [dɪu,dʒu—]: *n.* Ringworm on the feet, especially on the toes; athlete's foot; an infection caused by hookworm. Upcountry. In the Pee Dee this is called *foot itch.* Cf. DA: "a breaking-out or rash thought to have been caused by dew."

dickety-boo: *n.* A ghost or "hant"; a bugaboo. Sumter.

dogwood toothbrush: *n.* A device made by bending a green dogwood twig back and forth at one place until the fibers are thoroughly loosened. Then the twig is broken at this place, presenting two ends which are suitable for brushing the teeth. Soot from the open chimney was formerly used as an abrasive. Also called *stick toothbrush.* Cf. DA, *blackgum toothbrush,* which also is heard in South Carolina.

double fist: *n.* The size of the fists together. Used only as an expression of size: "As big as your *double fist.*"

double the fist: *v. phr.* To double one's fist is to challenge to fight.

double handful: *n.* As much as the two hands will hold. A measure of quantity.

dough roller: *n.* A rolling pin. Pee Dee and northern area.

dreen, reen, treen for *drain, rain, train,* etc. See Introduction.

drink muddy water: *v. phr., proverbial.* When one interferes with another's vision or stands in another's light, he is told that he has been *drinking muddy water.* If the intruder does not understand, and asks for an explanation, he is told that he has evidently been *drinking muddy water* since one cannot see through him. Darlington County.

dusk dark: *n.* Twilight. Sumter County.

egg cracking: *n.* Same as *egg picking, q.v.* Lancaster County.

egg picking: *n.* A custom of the Easter season in the Dutch Fork. This is a contest in which two opponents each hold an egg and strike or pick them together until one egg is cracked. The holder of the cracked egg is the loser. Contestants take great care in choosing their eggs. Stores are well provided with eggs for the season, and buyers test the eggs for hardness by tapping them against the front teeth. They can tell by the sound how strong the shell is. I have heard that the merchants charge a higher price per dozen if the buyer is allowed to choose his eggs. This practice has been recently reported. It is known also in Wisconsin and probably in Pennsylvania and elsewhere where Germans have settled.[4] [Common in Frederick County, Maryland and no doubt elsewhere in northwestern Maryland where Palatinate Germans settled. The challenge call goes something like "Who gotty egg?" the first word of which is shouted on a very high tone. The reply is, "I gotty egg!"—Ed.] DA, *egg pecking,* also current in S.C.

endearment, current terms of: sweetie pie, sugar dumpling, sugar foot, honey bun, honey bunch, honey chile, honey pie, sugar babe, sweet thing, sugar pie, little sugar.

English peas: *n. pl.* Garden peas, cultivated for table use. Also called *sugar peas* (Dutch Fork), *green peas, garden peas.* Not used in

---

[4] "Bei dem bekannten Eierpicken stoßen die Kinder ihre Ostereier mit dem spitzen Ende gegeneinander; wessen Ei zuerst zerbricht, der hat verloren. . . . Zu allem Eierspielen werden die Eier in festlichem Umzug gesammelt und nach dem Spiel aufgegessen." *Der Große Brockhaus, s.v. Eierfeste.*

the singular. Same as WNID, *pea*, 4. Not the variety of pea with edible pods, as WNID defines *sugar peas*. *English peas* are purveyed commercially and widely sold under the name *green peas*. All four of these terms are used generally in South Carolina, with the possible exception of *sugar peas*. DA, *English pea*.

Episcolopian: *n. and adj.* Episcopalian. EDD, *Episcolaupian*.

epizootics [ˌɛpɪˈzutɪks]: *n. pl.* Any disease of an animal, usually of a horse or mule, of indefinite nature. If an animal is "off his feed" or otherwise ailing for no known cause, it is said to have the *epizootics*. The term is also applied humorously to people. From *epizoötic*, through mispronunciation of the written or printed word. Cf. Wen. *epizootic* and *epizooty*, and WNID, *epizootic*.

evening piece: *n.* See *morning piece*.

eyeball: *n.* Someone dear, precious, especially a favorite child. "Dat chile 'e mammy *eyeball*." Also plural.

ficy, feisty [faɪsɪ, faɪstɪ]: *adj.* Same as Wen. and WNID, *feisty*, etc.

flapjack: *n.* An apple turnover fried in deep grease, also called *fried puppy* in Anderson County. This may also apply to turnovers made of other dried fruits, as peaches, apricots. The word is sometimes also applied to any pancake or griddle cake.

flat cake: *n.* A piece of biscuit dough flattened and baked on top of the stove. This is usually small, and baked for or by a child, but larger *flat cakes* have also been made in the same way. They are turned over and baked on both sides. Cf. DA, *flat bread*.

flimsy: *n.* Influenza. Folk etymology. Abbeville County.

flugins: *n. pl.* [ˈflugɪnz] In the phrases "cold as *flugins*" "cold as blue *flugins*." The various ways in which this word is used have in common only the fact that it is always an intensive. Not common, but still heard. Wen. gives the pronunciation [ˈfludʒɪnz], which I have never heard.

flyblow: *v.t.* To inform on, to report someone's bad conduct. An inebriated gentleman warned us boys: "Look here boys, don't you *flyblow* me." Cf. WNID, *flyblown*.

fly brush: *n.* A brush for keeping flies away, as from food on the table or otherwise. It consisted originally of a green, leafy branch, then of a long cane bedizened along one end for about two feet with colored tissue paper cut into strips. A mechanical *fly brush* was also used, with two revolving wings driven by a spring in the base. Still more elaborate affairs were swung from the ceiling and drawn back and forth by a string. The most glamorous *fly brushes*, used in the low country, were made of peacock feathers. Quite general before the coming of window and door screens. Obsolescent. Cf. Wen., *fly swat*. Same as DA, *fly brush*. Cf. *PADS*, No. 19, p. 10, *fly bresh*.

flying jinny: *n*. A merry-go-round consisting of a long board pivoted in the middle with a spike driven into the top of a post. One child sits on either end and a third child pushes it around. General.

fodderin' time: *n*. Time to pull fodder. Sumter County.

foot itch: *n*. See *dew poison*.

free seed: *n*. See *clear seed*.

fresh: *n*. Fresh meat; game. This has been reported from Wedge-field (*DN*, VI, 31), referring to butchered pork. In the low country it includes also game. "Sam, take yo' bag an' gun. We ain't had no *fresh* in I dunno when."

fried puppy: *n*. Same as *flapjack*.

gall: *n*. A low wooded area; an area overgrown with bushes or low trees, as a *muckle* (*myrtle*) *gall*. Eastern and coastal region. Cf. WNID, *gall*, n. 4, and EDD, *gall*, *sb.b*.

garden house: *n*. A privy. Also called *little house, necessary*. [For the distribution of this term, see H. Kurath, *A Word Geography of the Eastern United States* (Ann Arbor, 1949), p. 53 and F55.—Ed.]

gallices[-ɪ-]: *n. pl.* Galluses. A pronunciation of the Dutch Fork.

Georgia roll: *n*. A method of moving a heavy, oblong object, as a bale of cotton, by lifting one end, balancing it on the lower edge, and rotating it so that the lower end rolls on the ground.

giffy: *adj*. Of lumber, waterlogged and unfit for use. Charleston.

gillgadget: *n*. A thingumbob, a dingus. Chesterfield County. Wen., ATS.

gillhicket: *n*. Any small mechanical device, monkey wrench, special screwdriver, etc. Williamsburg County. ATS.

good dark: *adj*. As dark as it will get to be. *Good* is used here adverbially and intensively. Cf. DA, *good and*. Used with many other adjectives: *good done*, etc.

gopher scrape: *n*. A case of necessity, where one has to do what would otherwise be considered improper. Reported only from Williamsburg and Darlington Counties. Cf. Wen. *groundhog case*. The phrase is supposed to be derived from the following story: A preacher was coming to dinner one Sunday after the sermon, and two small boys were sent out to dig a gopher out of his hole for the preacher's dinner. The digging was in progress when the preacher himself came along and reproved the boys for working on the Sabbath. The boys' answer was: "We've got to get this gopher out of here for the preacher's dinner."

gormuck: *v.t.* To soil with grease, molasses or otherwise, as the hands, face, clothing. This seems to be a blend of *gorm* and *mummock*, *PADS*, No. 14, pp. 33, 48, both with approximately the same meaning. Charleston and coastal area.

grabble: *v.i.* To grope underwater along the banks of a stream to catch fish. "To *grabble* for cats."

grab hoe: *n.* A garden implement like a hoe, but with prongs instead of a blade. Sumter County. Local dealers sometimes call this a *grab rake.*

granny scrape: *n.* A birth in the family. "John is expecting a *granny scrape* at his house." *Granny* is rather generally used for a midwife.

graveyard widow: *n.* See *sod widow.*

greenglaze collards: *n.pl.* A variety of collards with a deep green color. This expression is well-known in the seed trade.

green peas: *n.pl.* See *English peas.*

Green Thursday: *n.* A Thursday in the Spring when housekeepers try to have green vegetables on the table. The expression has no religious implications. Dutch Fork. Cf. WNID.

gripegut: *n.* Same as *gruntler* below.

growel: *n.* A mule. Cf. G.P.W., *gowl*, a horse, which may be from German *Gaul.*

gruntler: *n.* One who is constantly complaining. Cf. WNID *gruntle, v.i.*, to grunt, to grumble. Obs. exc. dial. Lancaster County.

guinea watermelon: *n.* The same as *cymling*, q.v. Northern and eastern region.

gully buster: *n.* A heavy downpour of rain. Northern and eastern region. DA, *gullywasher.*

gumbo: *n.* Okra and tomatoes cooked together. WNID, a soup, thickened with the mucilagenous pods of okra.

haffers: *n.pl.* Lights of a slaughtered hog. Blythewood, Fairfield County. Mostly Negro usage.

half a sack: *n.* See under *shirtsleeve.*

hank, hink for *thank, think.* See Introduction.

hant's breath: *n*. A current of warm air felt out of doors in the evening, especially when riding on horseback or in a buggy. This is supposed also to be the *hant* itself, warm because from the lower regions. Low country.

harbis home: *n*. The time when the harvest has been gathered into the barn or otherwise under shelter. Pee Dee.

haul buggy: *v. phr*. To go away, to go home, to leave, especially in flight or in haste. Not necessarily in a buggy. Coastal, northern and northwestern region. Cf. *horse along* and *buggy along*, reported from Missouri, meaning to go on horseback or in a buggy.

heavy handed: *adj*. Extravagant. This applies especially to the kitchen: *heavy handed* with the butter, salt, sugar, etc., but not exclusively. One hears also "She has a *heavy hand* with. . . ." Cf. WNID.

hemstring: *n*. A *hamestring*. Pronunciation of Lancaster County.

high strikes: *n.pl*. Hysterics. Folk etymology. Only in such a phrase as "Isn't that enough to give you the *high strikes*?" Aiken County.

hill: *n*. Solid ground, as opposed to swamp. When timbers are moved out of the swamp they are said to be on the *hill* when they reach solid ground. EDD, *hill*, 5, a piece of high ground entirely surrounded by water; a dry patch of elevated marsh.

hitch out: *v.t*. To unhitch, as a horse from the plow, buggy, etc. The opposite of hitch up. EDD, *v*. 2, 8, *hitch* with *off* or *out*, to unharness, to release horses from work.

hnyah-hnyah: *adj*. Same as *squawed*, *q.v.* Chesterfield County.

hog choker: *n*. See *kiboka*.

holly loaf: *n*. An oblong loaf of bread formed by plaiting together strands of dough, used by Jewish families on the eve of the Seventh Day, symbolizing the Divine Presence. WNID, *hallah*, a kind of cake or bread used in certain sacrifices. This usage is probably known widely throughout the nation. Another form of this loaf, much larger and round, is used on special occasions, as on the Day of Atonement.

holy dancing: *n*. See *devil dancing*.

hominy snow: *n*. Snow in fine grains like hominy grits, as opposed to the large flakes. Not obsolete in South Carolina. Cf. DA.

horse: *v.i.* and *v.t*. To swagger about, to domineer. Cf. WNID *horse*, *v.t*. 7, to ridicule vigorously or savagely.

horse-necked jonquil: *n*. The daffodil, so called because of the way the flower arches its stem. Obsolescent. Also called *yellow trumpeter*. Charleston.

horsing: *pres. part., adj.* Rearing, as a fallen tree, supported by its branches so that it does not lie flat, but at an angle.

hot supper: *n.* A social gathering with provision of food (usually cold), at which the attendants entertained and amused themselves for hours. Originally the food was evidently served hot, but later, for convenience, it was served cold. Negro usage. Not recently heard.

hump along: *v.i.* To move swiftly, either on foot or in a vehicle. DA, *hump*; Wen., *hump to*.

hunk over: *v.t.* To hand over, with the connotation of misgiving, unwillingness; to fork over. Lancaster County.

hunker: *v.i.* To go, walk. Often with the adv. *along*, as in "I've got to *hunker* along."

jiggerboo: *n.* A Negro. Only in a derogatory sense. Not often heard, and evidently imported into South Carolina from other states. Returning servicemen report having heard it from various outside quarters. Wen., *jig*, 3.

ketch back: *v.i.* To return. Cf. WNID, *catch*, to chase; to hasten. Timmonsville and coastal area. Cf. *haul buggy*.

kiboka: *n.* "A small tough flounder or sole fish, called also *hog choker*. Small fish are caught with a seine and fed to the hogs, and this tough fish chokes them." Mount Pleasant.

kin: *n.* Dawn. A pronunciation of *can*. Only in the phrase "from *kin* to *kint*", i.e., from "can (see) to can't (see)," or from dawn to dark. Also, "*kin* to can't," "can to can't." Low country.

kint: *n.* See *kin*.

kite: *excl.* In the game of hide and seek, the one who "hides his eyes" while the others hide recites, "Ten, ten, double ten, forty-five, fifteen, one's a hundred—All ain't ready holler *kite*." Cf. Wen., *kite, v.i.*, to hurry. One hears also, "All ain't ready holler out," "All ain't ready holler I."

knocker: *n.* A small boy. Usually a *little knocker*. Sometimes depreciatory. Wen.

Lally's: *n.* Same as *lalla shop*, *PADS*, No. 14, p. 43. Charleston.

lamp oil times: *n.pl.* The old days. Charleston.

last while: *n.* The immediate past. "We haven't had rain for the *last while*."

latch pin: *n.* 1. A safety pin. Cf. *PADS*, No. 19, p. 12. 2. The homemade wooden bolt inside the door lifted by the latch string.

leg rip: *n.* La grippe. Folk etymology. Abbeville County.

less mo': *adv.* Much less. "He can't stand up, *less mo'* walk."

lie-low: *n.* In the expression: A *lie-low* to catch meddlers. See G.P.W., pp. 557–558, where a large number of variants are cited.

light a shuck, light a rag: *v. phr.* To move away in haste.

limb of Satan: *n.* A wicked, vicious person. EDD.

limpin' Katie, limpin' Kate, limpin' Kit, skippin' Jinny: *n.* Originally, cowpeas and hominy cooked separately and eaten together. Other reports have it that the cowpeas and hominy were cooked together.[5] Cf. *PADS*, No. 14, p. 45.

limpin' Susan: *n.* Okra pilau, a dish made of chopped bacon, okra, rice, and seasoning. Charleston.

liter [ˈlaɪtɚ, ˈlaɪtə]: *v.i.* Loiter. Cf. *pint* for *point*, *jint* for *joint*, etc. Chesterfield County.

little house: *n.* See *garden house, necessary*.

liver: *n.* An inhabitant, dweller. "He de oldes' *liver* on dis block." Negro usage, Charleston and Sumter.

liver nips: *n.pl.* A viand prepared with a base of ground or minced beef liver highly seasoned with onions, pepper, and many other ingredients. There are many varying receipts. A favorite dish in the Dutch Fork.

---

[5] The following letter from Rowesville is of interest: "I was born in 1873 and am now seventy-eight years old. My father ran a farm—an eight or ten horse farm—could get labor cheap in those days. I came in before the hard years of Reconstruction were ended, so I knew how to save and be thrifty. My father tried to raise about all of our food except sugar and coffee. Our rice was hulled in a mortar, which was a log about eight feet high, hollowed out about two feet, and would contain about one-half bushel of unhulled rice. A pestle was used to pound or beat the rice, raising it up and dropping it back in the mortar, up and down, until the husk would begin to come off. This was then taken out and put in a sifter and winnowed. The chaff came out, then it was put back and strips of shuck were put in to bleach or whiten the rice. After a lot of fanning it was ready to use. One of the farm hands would beat it for my mother. This one in particular could or would get it cleaner than the others. Well sometimes the housewife found her rice out. Her pot of peas was on cooking and no rice. Hands all in the field, no time to stop and beat rice. Saturday was rice-beating day. So a pot of grits was the answer. The family had to eat. So my mother would say to her help: 'Well, Mary we will have *limping Katie* today.' The hominy had to be limp or soft to get that name. So *limping Katie* is hominy and peas, but not cooked together."

live the life: *v. phr.* To live a blameless life, above reproach. The phrase has religious overtones. Sumter county.

make out one's meal: *v.phr.* 1. To eat heartily, as when a guest is urged to *make out his meal.* Dutch Fork. 2. To eke out one's meal, as, when there is a scarcity of one dish, to *make out one's meal* on other dishes. "That is all of the hash. You'll have to *make out your meal* on turnip greens and cornbread." General.

malahack: *n.* Ballyhack or ballywack, as in Wen. Pee Dee. Cf. EDD, *malahack,* to cut or carve in an awkward way.

midgin': *adj.* Middlin', especially in greetings. "How do you feel today?" "Just *midgin'.*" Summerville.

miller's rule: *n.* The miller's rule is that everyone comes in his turn, and each one must await his turn.

miss-meal colic: *n.* Hunger. A variant of *missed-meal colic. PADS,* No. 14, p. 46.

mixed bread: *n.* A bread made up of flour, mush or hominy, yeast, and various seasonings according to local tradition. Known and prized in Newberry, Lexington, Fairfield, Richland, and Saluda Counties. Product of the Dutch Fork.

molasses jug: *n.* Same as *brown jug, q.v.*

morning piece: *n.* A layout of coffee, tea, or other beverage with crackers, cookies, or sandwiches offered to morning callers. *Evening piece* is a similar offering in the afternoon or evening.

mought: *v.* Might. This is still heard in South Carolina. It may be obsolescent, as Wen. indicates. Nonstandard usage.

muckle gall, cane gall, etc.: See *gall.*

mudder: *n.* Mother. This may be a survival of *moder* and hence a form historically warranted. EDD (Westmorland and Cumberland)

necessary: *n.* A euphemism for *backhouse.* See also *garden house, little house.* [For distribution of this term, also current in the Boston area, see Kurath, *A Word Geography of the Eastern United States,* p. 53 and F55.—Ed.]

nips [nɪps, nɛps]: *n.pl.* Small spoon dumplings, i.e., dumplings made by dropping the dough into the pot with a spoon. The pronunciation [nɛps] is confined to the Dutch Fork.

norate: *v.t.* To depreciate. Usually of persons. Cf. Wen., EDD. [?Blend of *narrate* and *low-rate.* Cf. *PADS,* No. 14, p. 45, *low-rate.* —Ed.]

October flowers: *n.pl.* Chrysanthemums. Also *Octobers.*

open stone: *adj.* See *clear seed.*

part the bedclothes, divide the bedclothes: *v.phr.* Of a married couple: to separate. Anderson County. The phrase to *split blankets* (*q.v.*) is used in the same way. These expressions are not common, but are still used.

physic: *n.* A ridiculous sight. Perhaps from the therapeutic value of laughter. Dutch Fork.

pickpoke: *n.* A cotton picker's sack. Cherokee County.

piece: *v.t.* To make, as a quilt. Used only in this connection and derived from the *piecing* together of a crazy quilt. Dutch Fork.

pigeon pair: *n.* A boy and girl, usually brother and sister, close enough in age to be congenial playmates. Cf. EDD, *pigeon's pair,* a family consisting of a son and a daughter only.

pigeonwing: *n.* a type of dance involving the use of the arms. Cf. DA.

pine blank: *adj.* Direct; bold; shameless; especially in the phrase: A *pine blank* lie or liar, but also in other phrases: "I swear *pine blank.*" From *point blank, pint blank.*

piney woods rooter, pine rooter: *n.* A hog turned out to find his living by *rooting* in the woods, long-snouted, thin, razor-backed.

piroot: *v.i.* To nose around, to "peruse" around, where one has no business. Always with a connotation of derogation or contempt, and usually in the phrase: *pirootin' around.* "She got no call to come *pirootin' around* my husban'." Wen.

poke dinner: *n.* A lunch carried to work in a paper bag. Lancaster County.

pond chicken: *n.* Green frog, *rana catesbeiana.* Probably so called because of the edible hind legs, considered a delicacy. Williamsburg County and probably general along the coast.

posse cumtatum [ˈpɑsɪ kʌmˈtetəm]: *n.* A corruption of *posse comitatus.*[6] Sumter County.

pot hound: *n.* A hound which hunts nothing but the pot, i.e., is good for nothing but to eat; a worthless hound. DA.

potty: *adj.* Dirty, especially of children and their clothes. *Potty*

---

[6] [It is noteworthy that the "corruption" reported by Dean Bradley preserves English [-e-] in the penultimate syllable of *comitatus.* A "little learning" has caused most speakers schooled in the "reformed" pronunciation of Latin, presumably more "correct" than the traditional, to say [ˈpɑsɪ ˌkomɪˈtɑtəs]. Here, as frequently, traces of a cultivated pronunciation of the past linger on in the speech of the folk.—Ed.]

black is often heard. Probably from the iron pot which sat on the stove or over an open fire. Apparently not related to WNID, *potty*, insignificant.

pretty hands: *n.pl.* The hands folded as in prayer. Used in speaking to or of children. While the blessing is being asked, children are told: "Make *pretty hands!*" Mostly in the upcountry, and apparently not quite general there.

primp: *v.i.* To distort the face, as a child beginning to cry. Cf. WNID, *prim, v.* 1, and *primp, v.* 2, also EDD, *prim, v.*

project [ˈprɑdʒɪk]: *v.i.* To play; to trifle; to tinker; to project with something. "They were *projecting* with a pistol and it went off." To loiter, to idle about in aimless search of something pleasant or easy to do. "I'm just *projectin'* around." Cf. WNID *project, v.*, 2 and 3. DA and Wen. list this word but do not indicate the accent on the penult.

pull one's cap: *v.phr.* To tip or pull the cap in greeting a lady, also out of respect for an older person.

pull wool: *v.phr.* To pluck at one's forelock in "bowing and scraping." Formerly of Negroes, now obsolete. Cf. WNID, *leg, n.* 4.

quizbag: *n.* A meddler; an obnoxious person. Dutch Fork. Cf. WNID, *quiz, v.* 1.

rare out: *v.t.* Same as *bless out.* Dutch Fork. Cf. Wen., *rare,* to rant, to fuss, etc., and WNID, *rear, v.i.* and EDD, *rear,* 11, to mock, jibe, scold.

reverend: *adj.* Pure, in full strength. To take one's coffee *reverend* is to take it without cream or sugar; applied also to whiskey, neat. DA.

riz biscuits: *n.pl.* Yeast rolls. Dutch Fork. Sporadic in Pee Dee and Upcountry.

riz bread: *n.* Light bread. Dutch Fork. Sporadic in the Pee Dee and upcountry.

rock stone: *n.* A stone. Wadmalaw Island.

rooster: *v.i.* To act in a cocky manner; to swagger. "To go *roosterin'* around."

roundabout: *n.* Rounders (WNID *rounder,* 6) A boys' baseball game. See *PADS*, No. 14, p. 57. Also called *scrubahole.*

rounders: *n.pl.* The gid, coenurosis. A disease of sheep that causes them to move in circles.

rumpspringing: *pres. part., n.* Of a skirt, the act of bagging in the seat, caused by sitting. An inner lining is sometimes used to prevent *rumpspringing*. Cf. *buttbroke*.

rumpsprung: *adj.* See preceding.

same and same: *adj.phr.* Exactly alike. Same as *ting an' ting*, *PADS*, No. 14, p. 67.

samp: *n.* Hulled corn. Lower S. C. In the upcountry this is usually called *big hominy* or *lye hominy*. Purveyed in tin cans, it is called in the trade *hominy*. Cf. WNID.

sapphire grass: *n.* The *liriope spicata*. So called because of the *sapphire* berries at its base. Brought presumably from China, it is also called *China grass*. Its long slender leaves drooping down to the ground may be the origin of another name, *snake whiskers*, applied to it. It forms a favorite evergreen border.

sapsucker: *n.* Of a person, a term of contempt.

savannah: *n.* A small highland pond. Sumter County.

school breaking: *n.* Same as *school exhibition*.

school exhibition: *n.* A public entertainment marking the end of the school year. It consists of songs, dialogues, short plays, recitations, declamations, broom drills, and the like. In the eighties and nineties these exhibitions were a social event of first importance in the community. Cf. DA, *school entertainment*.

sconch: *v.t.* To scotch or squelch, as a rumor. Cf. EDD, *squanch*, to quench. Lancaster County.

scrubahole: *n.* Same as *roundabout*.

scudder, scutter: *n.* A small boy. Almost always *little scudder*. Cf. Wen., *scud, scutter*.

seed wart: *n.* A wart which shows the seed-like papillae on its surface.

shad-bellied: *adj.* Narrow at the ends and wide in the middle; said of lumber incorrectly sawed.

shagra hominy: *n.* Coarse ground grits cooked to a grainy consistency. Greenwood County. See WNID, *samp*.

shake a funky sock, *v.phr.* To dance. Low. For *funky*, which is fairly general in the South, see Wen. The body odor of vigorous dancers accounts for this usage.

shanksprung: *past part., adj.* Bow-legged.

shelly beans, shellies: *n.pl.* Beans gathered late in the season, too mature and tough to be cooked in the pod as string beans. They are shelled out and cooked with other string beans that are not too tough. Cf. Wen. and *PADS*, No. 19, p. 13. Spartanburg County.

shine: *intensive.* "Are you scared of him?" "*Shine* no!" "Can you lick him?" "*Shine* yes, I can lick hell out of him!" Quite common in the eastern corner of the State. Sporadic in other parts. EDD, *shine*, entirely, utterly (This is given in a supplementary list at the beginning of Vol. V "for want of information.")

shingle: *v.t.* To cut the hair awkwardly, so that it has the appearance of shingles on a roof. In the eighties and nineties, when barber shops were not easily accessible, the members of a family often had their hair cut in the home by someone willing to undertake the task. This saved the price of a haircut in a barber shop, but often resulted in *shingling.* ?Obsolete. Not recently observed. Cf. WNID, *shingle*, *v.t.* 2, to cut or bob the hair so close that the contour, especially of the back of the head, is clearly brought out. Also DA.

shirtsleeve: *n.* A ten-pound sack of flour. The twenty-four pound sack is called a *bootleg*, the forty-eight pound sack is *half a sack*, and the ninety-six pound sack is called a *sack* of flour. More recently the weights are: 10, 25, 50, and 100.

shivering owl: *n.* A screech owl.

shrimp mammy: *n.* A squid, often caught in the net with shrimp. Coastal area.

shuck beans: *n.pl.* Beans picked green and strung on twine, partly dehydrated in the oven and hung out for further drying. They are stored for use in winter. Soaked in water overnight, they are boiled with ham bone or other pork. Same as *leather breeches, PADS*, No. 14, p. 44, and *shelly beans*, above. Wen.

shucky beans: *n.pl.* Beans too mature to be eaten as snap beans or string beans. The pod when chewed leaves an unpalatable shucky residue. Cf. Wen., *shuck beans, shucky beans*, and *PADS*, No. 19, p. 14, *shucky beans.*

s'I, s'e: *phr.* Said I, said he. Not so common as *sez I, sez 'e*, but still heard.

sigodlin: *adj.* Same as *squawed*, *q.v.* Chesterfield County. Wen.

sirey ['saɪrɪ]: *adj.* Sorry, worthless. "He's a *sirey* rascal." Northern section of the State.

skeet: *v.i.* and *v.t.* To spurt water or saliva between the teeth. "To *skeet* ambeer," to squirt tobacco spittle between the teeth. Cf. Wen., EDD, *skeet*, *v.*, to eject saliva through the teeth.

skipping Jack: *n.* Left-over hoppin' john [See *PADS*, No. 14, p. 38.—Ed.], fried for breakfast the next morning. Charleston.

snake whiskers: *n.pl.* See *sapphire grass.*

sneck: *n.* A latch or fastening. WNID; obs. except Scot. and dial. Lancaster County.

snits: *n.pl.* Fruit, usually apples or peaches, cut up unpeeled and dried in the sun. This seems to differ from *snits, schnits* as reported in Wen., in that the fruit is unpeeled. Dutch Fork.

snits: *n.* A young, inexperienced person, not "dry behind the ears." Contemptuous. Probably from *snits*, fruit cut small. Dutch Fork.

snouse: *v.i.* To rummage around in another's belongings without permission, on the sly. Perhaps a blend of *snoop* and *browse.* Dutch Fork.

snub, snuff: *v.i.* To sob involuntarily after a fit of crying. Usually of children. Wen., *snub.* EDD, *snob*, to sob; *snuff*, to sniff.

sod widow, graveyard widow: *n.* One whose husband is dead; not a grass widow.

sough [su]: *v.i.* To whistle, as wind or water. WNID [sʌf, saʊ], EDD, *soo*, a whistling sound, the sound of the wind or water. Northeastern part of the State.

span, spin: *n.* Seminal fluid. *Span* is a pronunciation heard mostly from Negroes.

spin: *v.i.* To eject seminal fluid. Probably related to *spean, v.i.*

split blankets: *v.phr.* See *part the bedclothes.*

spean: *v.t.* and *v.i.* 1. To milk, as a cow. Northern and eastern section. 2. To spurt out in a fine stream, especially said of the teats of a milk cow. "The cow's bag was so full the milk was *speaning* out." Cf. WNID, EDD, *spean, sb.*, the teat of any female animal, especially a cow.

spoon dumplings: *n.pl.* See *nips.* Dutch Fork.

sprockle: *v.i.* To try hard for something difficult to obtain; to make a great effort. Cf. WNID, *sprauchle*, to clamber, scramble, sprawl. Scot., N. of Eng., and Ireland; *sprack, adj.*, active; alert; alive; nimble; shrewd; deft. All chiefly Scot. and dial. Eng. Lancaster County.

squawed: *past part., adj.* Out of plumb, said of a door or window frame, house, or other construction when warped or careened out of the rectangular shape or vertical position. Used mostly by builders. Apparently stemming from Hartsville, where it may have been imported from northeastern North Carolina, it has spread to Beaufort County, Lancaster County, and a few other localities,

but is not in general use over the state.[7] It is known in Chesterfield County, where also several other synonymous expressions are
used: *whonkum*, *sigodlin*, *antigodlin*, *hnyah-hnyah*, the last with
strong nasalization.

stepney: *n.* Extremely hard times, starvation times; hunger.
Coastal area. *"Stepney* ain' fuh come een my house." Ambrose
Gonzales, *The Black Border* (1922), p. 34. *Stepney* is also looked
upon as an evil spirit or "hant."

stick toothbrush: *n.* See *dogwood toothbrush.*

straw field: *n.* A field, usually of wornout land, overgrown with
broom sedge. Also called *broomstraw field.*

stumpy broom, stub broom: *n.* A broom of straw worn down so
as to be of no use in sweeping the floor. Used to sweep the yard.

sugar peas: *n.pl.* See *English peas.* WNID, a variety of pea with
edible pods.

sweet poison: *n.* A mixture of molasses, arsenic, and water for
poisoning boll weevils.

swigger: *v.i.* Euphemism for swear; "Well, I *swigger!*" General.
Wen. reports only "I'll be *swiggered!*"

swinge cat: *n.* A person of no morals; a wretched, pitiful creature.
Low country. See *PADS*, No. 14, p. 66.

swonger: *v.i.* To saunter, to stroll. Cf. EDD, *swank*, to strut
consequentially, to swagger.

swonger: *adj.* Exuberant; proud; haughty. Gullah.

syrup biscuit: *n.* A biscuit with a hole punched into the edge with
a finger and filled with syrup. Same as *molasses biscuit.*

tabor: *n.* A hymnal. Dutch Fork.

tecky: *excl.* Take care! Children are warned against danger thus:
"Tecky, tecky!" Gullah.

tenement: *n.* An apartment in a dormitory of several stories
comprising all the rooms to be reached through one front door.
Used, so far as is known, only on the campus of the University of
South Carolina. A *tenement* consists usually of six or eight study

---

[7] Mrs. H. F. Gregory writes from Beaufort, S.C.: "I am a Virginian by
birth, and have lived near Elizabeth City, N.C., for about twenty-nine
years. Off and on we moved here (Beaufort, S.C.) to work. The term
'squawed' is used there (in Elizabeth City) in reference to buildings, etc.,
out of shape. I do know that the term has been used here among the natives
of northeastern N.C. who have moved here."

rooms and about twelve bedrooms, and accommodates about twenty students.

'totin's: *n.pl.* See *carry*, n.

tough-mouthed, tough-mouthted: *past part., adj.* Having a tough mouth, inured to the bit. A young animal, horse or mule, has a tender, sensitive mouth. For the second form, cf. *drownded*, etc.

up the road: *adv. phr.* Up north. Negro usage.

vence: *interj.* Same as *venture, PADS,* No. 14, p. 70. Anderson County.

vinegar mammy: *n.* Mother of vinegar, *mycoderma aceti.*

wages hand: *n.* A wage laborer. DA, *wage worker.*

wagoner bread: *n.* Same as *flat cake.* Said to be named for the North Carolina wagoners who used to peddle tobacco, and who made this bread.

wampus kitty [ˈwɔmpəs ˈkɪtɪ]: *n.* A variant of *wampus cat, PADS,* No. 14, p. 70. Low country.

wastin': *present part., adj.* Having uterine bleeding. Negro usage.

water dog: *n.* A small patch, a short strip of rainbow. EDD defines *water dog* as various cloud effects said to presage rain; *water gall,* as a fragment of rainbow appearing on the horizon.

water gap: *n.* A structure of posts or stakes across a stream, joining with a fence on either side to prevent cattle from getting out of the pasture by walking in the channel. Cf. Wen., *gap* 5, a gate. Cf. DA, *water fence.*

which, the which, 'n' the which: *rel. pron.* The redundant use of *which* is well illustrated by Wen. In South Carolina this is more often *the which, 'n'* (and) *the which. The which* appears to be felt as a more proper form than *which.* "We are taking the kids to the circus tomorrow, *'n' the which* they haven't talked about nothing else but the circus for a month." "Paw told me to shut the gate, *the which* I had already shut it."[8]

---

[8] In *King Richard II* V. iii. 5–12, Bolingbroke says of his dissolute son:
Inquire at London, 'mongst the taverns there,
For there they say, he daily doth frequent,
With unrestrained loose companions,
Even such, they say, as stand in narrow lanes,
And beat our watch, and rob our passengers;
Which he, young wanton and effiminate boy,
Takes on the point of honor to support
So dissolute a crew.

whonkum: *adj.* Same as *squawed*, *q.v.* Chesterfield County.

wild asparagus: *n.* The tender shoots of the bull briar, purveyed in season in bunches and used as a vegetable. It is also called *chaney briar*. Charleston.

windlebit: *n.* A brace and bit. Dutch Fork. Cf. WNID *wimble*, *n.*, *windle.*, *n.*; EDD, *windle.*

woods chillun: *n.pl.* Illegitimate children. Also, *straw field chillun, bush chillun.* Cf. *woods colt, 'long-o-de-paat chillun, ditch-edge chillun,* all listed in *PADS*, No. 14.

woof [wuf] **at:** *v.t.* To address roughly, rudely. Cf. WNID *woof*, *n.*, and *wough*, *v.i.*

yard broom: *n.* See *brush broom*.

yellow trumpeter: *n.* See *horse-necked jonquil*.

THE SECRETARY'S REPORT

A. THE CHICAGO MEETING

The annual meeting of the Society was held at the Palmer House in Chicago, December 28, 1953, 9:00–10:30 A.M., with approximately 75 persons attending. The following papers were read:

1. "Eastern Dialect Words in California," David W. Reed, University of California, Berkeley.

2. "A Lexicographical Note," Louise Pound, University of Nebraska.

3. "Dialect Differentiation in the Stories of Joel Chandler Harris," Sumner Ives, Tulane University.

The report of the Nominating Committee (B. J. Whiting, Chairman; Marjorie Kimmerle, C. M. Wise) was read by Atcheson L. Hench and accepted by the members present. James B. McMillan, Levette J. Davidson, and Thomas Pyles were reëlected President, Vice-President, and Secretary-Treasurer respectively. Karl W. Dykema, who was elected to the Executive Council in December, 1952, to replace Professor McMillan for a term expiring in December, 1953, was reëlected for a full term expiring in December, 1957.

Edward Artin read the report of the Auditor (Ernest H. Cox), which was accepted.

Levette J. Davidson read Chairman Margaret M. Bryant's report of the Research Committee on Proverbial Sayings, as follows:

Collecting of proverbial sayings still continues. Professor Herbert Halpert writes that a student of his made a good East Tennessee collection of proverbial comparisons, to be published in the *Tennessee Folklore Society Bulletin*. Professor Muriel J. Hughes had a grant from the University of Vermont for collecting and studying the folk sayings of that state.

California, however, is leading in the amount of work being done on proverbial sayings. California's final count, according to Professor Wayland Hand (Chairman), is 22,000. The material is to appear in three volumes: (1) proverbial comparisons, (2) proverbs, (3) proverbial phrases. The first of the three volumes, *Proverbial Comparisons and Similes from California*, about 100 pages, is now in page proof, and will be published early in 1954 by the University of California Press, edited by Professor Archer Taylor. Professor Taylor is also editing the volume of proverbs and Professor G. O. Arlt the volume of proverbial phrases, both of which are well under way.

42

Before too long California will have the proverbial material published. It is to be hoped that other states will rapidly follow in her footsteps.

I. Willis Russell, Chairman of the Research Committee on New Words, reported as follows:

Again this year, for the eleventh time, the Committee prepared the article "Words and Meanings, New" for the *Britannica Book of the Year*. As usual the Chairman was ably assisted by his committee members, who supplied citations, framed definitions, and did extensive checking. The Committee consists of Henry Alexander (Queen's University), Thomas L. Crowell (Columbia University), O. B. Emerson (University of Alabama), Atcheson L. Hench (University of Virginia), Mamie J. Meredith (University of Nebraska), and Peter Tamony (San Francisco).

In the absence of Albert H. Marckwardt, Chairman of the Research Committee on Linguistic Geography, Raven I. McDavid, Jr., reported for that Committee as follows:

During 1953 American scholars have continued to show their interest in linguistic geography by initiating new projects, developing projects already undertaken, and preparing derivative studies based on existing collections.

1. Hans Kurath, Director of the Linguistic Atlas of the United States and Canada, reports continuing steady sales of the *Linguistic Atlas of New England* and the accompanying *Handbook*. In fact, the first edition of the *Handbook* has now been exhausted, and a second edition authorized by the ACLS, sponsors of the Atlas project.

The materials from the Middle and South Atlantic States are on file at the University of Michigan. Plans for editing these materials have been ready for some time, but as yet no funds for editing are available. The ACLS is continuing to look for funds. In the meantime, many scholars have made use of the *Atlas* collections, and many important derivative studies have been undertaken. Kurath's *Word Geography of the Eastern United States*, the first of these studies, has sold 1600 copies. The second, Atwood's *Survey of Verb Forms of the Eastern United States*, has received very favorable reviews. The third, *The Pronunciation of English in the Eastern United States*, by Kurath and R. I. McDavid, Jr., is largely in first draft; McDavid has been granted an MLA subvention to assist in completing the MS (he has summarized a part of the data for this study in "Pronunciation Patterns in the Historical South," a paper presented in April, 1953, at the Sixth Kentucky Foreign Language Conference). A fourth such study, Mrs. Virginia McDavid's analysis of regional and social patterns in the grammar of spoken American English, is scheduled for completion in 1954 as a University of Minnesota dissertation; it will also use data from the North-Central and Upper Midwest regional surveys. Besides these studies six Michigan dissertations in preparation are using materials from the Atlas collections, as follows:

Walter S. Avis, The In-Gliding Mid Vowels, as in *road* and *take*.

James Downer, The Dialect of the Biglow Papers.

William Van Riper, Post-vocalic /-r/ in the Eastern States.

Thomas Wetmore, The Low-Back Vowels as in *cost, fog, water, daughter*, etc.

Mrs. J. V. Williamson, Negro Speech of Memphis, Tennessee.

Helen Wong, The high-back vowels as in *room, roof, root*, etc.

2. The collections of the Linguistic Atlas of the North-Central States are nearing completion under the direction of A. H. Marckwardt (also at Michigan), despite special problems in Indiana and Kentucky. In Indiana, Byron W. Bender, who began work in 1950, was unable to find time for intensive field trips because of other academic commitments; when he abandoned field work for a linguistic investigation in the Marshall Islands in the summer of 1953, he had completed 23 field records, several of them fragmentary, and reported having tape recordings of eleven other interviews. Nine of these tapes he has since returned to the University of Indiana for transcribing. A new field worker was incapacitated by an eye operation; a third is now transcribing Bender's tapes and completing the twelve or fifteen interviews that remain to be done in Indiana. From the Indiana experience we may draw several valuable lessons:

a. A field worker must have uninterrupted blocks of time for his field trips. In six months of steady field work he can do more than he could in three years of part-time operations.

b. A new field worker should draw upon the experience of his predecessors; a joint interview provides invaluable training in handling informants, manipulating the questionnaire, and becoming alert to the conversational forms which provide the most useful data for grammatical studies.

c. If the field worker uses tapes, he should nevertheless make his impressionistic transcription during the live interview. Tapes are invaluable as a source of supplementary grammatical and phonological data, as a record of the difficult phenomena of stress, intonation, and juncture, and as a permanent record of the entire interview. But trusting in the tape alone means that the field worker must spend many valuable hours manipulating the tapes to find the data he could have recorded on the spot.

Unlike Indiana, Kentucky has available field workers but no funds to support them. No local institution or agency has contributed any financial assistance to the work of the *Atlas*. Nineteen interviews—a third of the state—have been completed with funds from the University of Michigan, which has agreed to finance nine more interviews. Indiana University has promised to support at least ten interviews in central Kentucky. Since little more than a thousand dollars is needed to complete the Kentucky work, appeals have been made to several institutions in the North-Central area.

A grant from Western Reserve University has made possible several additional interviews in Ohio.

To supplement the field records, a check list has been prepared for distribution in the North-Central area. So far it is being used by Western Reserve, Ohio State, Ohio Wesleyan, and Ohio Universities, and Murray (Kentucky) State College. Other institutions are invited to make use of it.

By arrangement with Professor Marckwardt a deputy headquarters is now being set up Western Reserve University; it is hoped that ultimately this deputy headquarters will contain copies of all the North-Central field records, as well as copies of the Middle Atlantic field records for Ohio. Tentatively, this deputy headquarters will devote itself to (a) an analysis of the Ohio materials, (b) the study of pronunciation in the North-Central States. McDavid presented a preliminary survey of pronunciation patterns in the North-Central States at the 1953 meeting of the Speech Association of America.

3. From the Upper Midwest, Harold B. Allen of Minnesota reports the completion of field work in Nebraska, leaving only three field records to be done in St. Paul and Minneapolis before his field materials are complete. His file of completed check lists has passed 900, with a goal of a thousand from the five-state area of Minnesota, Iowa, the Dakotas, and Nebraska. Plans for editing and publishing are still incomplete; meanwhile, Allen has presented preliminary analyses of his findings at meetings of the Linguistic Society and the MLA.

4. In the Rocky Mountain area, Marjorie Kimmerle, director of the Rocky Mountain Atlas, has completed the Colorado field work, with assistance from Allan Hubbell of Denver and Mrs. Etholine Aycock of Colorado State. Editorial work has begun, with the help of a grant from the research funds of the University of Colorado, but has progressed slowly because of Miss Kimmerle's recent illness. John McKendrick of Brigham Young University expects to complete the Utah field work by May, as part of a Johns Hopkins University dissertation. Work in Montana has remained dormant since 1951; Louis Milic of Montana State College has recently assumed responsibility for completing the field work and for enlarging the file of check lists. In New Mexico, Donald Dickinson has completed seven field records for his M.A. thesis, and T. M. Pearce has engaged in several supplementary studies. Plans for Arizona and Wyoming are so far uncertain.

5. The Pacific Coast. Under the direction of David W. Reed of California, 87 field interviews have been completed of 300 projected in California and Nevada, as follows:

	Projected	Completed
San Francisco	25	25
Los Angeles	55	25
Oakland-East Bay	20	6
San Diego	8	6
Other California	162	22
Nevada	30	3
	300	87

The file of check lists from California and Nevada now totals slightly over 600, out of 1500 planned. So far, Northern California is better represented than the southern part of the state, and no check lists have been distributed in Nevada.

One dissertation has been completed, based on the Pacific Coast material —The Pronunciation of English in San Francisco, by David DeCamp.

Preliminary work has been done in Washington by Carroll Reed of the University of Washington. Henry Person of Washington is now distributing a new check list. So far, however, no field work has been undertaken in Washington or Oregon, or in British Columbia, where A. W. DeGroot of the University of British Columbia has indicated a desire to cooperate in the project. DeCamp is now a member of the faculty of Washington State College (Pullman) and expects to get support for field work in Idaho and Eastern Washington.

6. Texas and the Gulf States. In Texas, as in Kentucky, investigators have found difficulty in translating local patriotism and interest in local culture into the support needed for a systematic investigation. The only systematic work accomplished so far has been an investigation by check lists sent out by E. B. Atwood of the University of Texas; a preliminary report appeared in the latest issue of *Orbis*.

In the past two decades students of C. M. Wise at Louisiana State have made over a hundred field records in Louisiana and parts of neighboring states; this work continues. These records provide valuable preliminary information and much data unobtainable elsewhere.

More recently, J. B. McMillan of Alabama and Sumner Ives of Tulane have taken steps toward a systematic investigation of Gulf States speech. Ives has put on tape many brief samples of New Orleans speech, which reveal the complexity of regional and social patterns in the Lower Mississippi and the need for carefully choosing informants. He is now coöperating with the Urban Research Center of New Orleans in studying the correlation between language patterns and social status.

7. Canada. In 1952 a conference was held at the University of Toronto to promote research in Canadian English. The Rev. Bro. Pius (George Conlin) is conducting a check-list survey of Eastern Ontario. H. M. Alexander's survey of the Maritime Provinces has not been resumed since the war; in 1951, H. R. Wilson, of Augustana College, began a more intensive survey of Queens County, Nova Scotia.

8. The Central States. George Pace, of the University of Missouri, has recently inaugurated a series of masters' theses in the vocabulary of Missouri counties, utilizing a modification of Allen's check list for the Upper Midwest. For these theses the county is taken as the unit, following the pattern of Robert Ramsay's series of place-name studies. Field work lies in the future. Nothing has been reported from Arkansas, Kansas, or Oklahoma.

9. Foreign-language communites. Einar Haugen of Wisconsin published his monumental *The Norwegian Language in America*, a work significant not only for the dialect data but also for the light it throws on problems of dialect mixture, linguistic borrowing, bilingualism, and culture change. Carroll Reed of Washington is now in Germany on a Fulbright Fellowship, investigating German dialects and the archives of the *Sprachatlas* as a preliminary step towards publishing the data he has collected for the Linguistic Atlas of Pennsylvania German.

11. One other study should be mentioned. The American Dialect Society has published (*PADS*, No. 20) the questionnaire used by F. G. Cassidy

for collecting lexical data in Wisconsin. This questionnaire should serve as a guide for other scholars interested in collecting systematic data towards a dictionary of American folk speech.

At no time in the past year—or for many years, for that matter—has there been either adequate financial support for research or an adequate number of trained investigators. In fact, only at California and Michigan have investigators been able to secure long-term support as a matter of institutional policy. This situation contrasts lamentably with that in such a country as Finland, which has not only rebuilt her economy and paid off crushing war indemnities but has been able to keep a number of full-time investigators in the field at decent, tax-free salaries. In view of our handicaps, we must admire the energy and devotion of those American scholars whose activities are giving us ever fuller and more accurate statements about American speech than we have previously had.

At the conclusion of Professor McDavid's report, Professor Pearce moved that, in appreciation of Professor Kimmerle's work in dialectology in the Rocky Mountain region, the Society express its best wishes for a speedy recovery from her recent illness. The motion was enthusiastically received, seconded, and passed. The Secretary has written Miss Kimmerle to that effect.

B. THE EXECUTIVE COUNCIL

Immediately preceding the annual meeting of the Society, a meeting of the Executive Council was held, with Messrs. McMillan, Davidson, Dykema, and the Secretary present. The Council appointed new chairmen (their names will be found on the inside front cover) of those research committees whose chairmanships have recently fallen vacant, and voted to abolish temporarily one research committee which has long been inactive.

The Council also voted to accept the generous offer of the University of Wisconsin to provide a fireproof repository for a number of complete files of *Dialect Notes* and the *Publication of the American Dialect Society*, as well as for any valuable collections that may come to the Society. The matter of a safe repository was initiated during Dean E. H. Criswell's tenure as President of the Society. Two copies of each issue of our publications from 1890 to the present have now been sent to the University of Wisconsin Library.

C. MEMBERSHIP

As of December 14, 1953, our membership stands as follows: Life, 15; Annual, 337; Libraries, 198; a total of 545.

D. FINANCES

Account from December 17, 1952 to December 14, 1953

Balance from 1952—		$1,099.71
Receipts		
From persons	$769.00	
From libraries	522.80	
Miscellaneous	758.07	
Total receipts		$2,049.87
Total of 1952 balance and 1952–53 receipts		$3,149.58
Disbursements		$ 927.16
Balance		$2,222.42

E. DEATHS

A. Stanley Umpleby, Honorary Secretary of the Yorkshire Dialect Society, probably in April. ("A month or two ago," according to a letter from his successor, Professor F. W. Moody, dated 1st June). Mr. Umpleby, a dialect poet of considerable merit, was preparing a dialect glossary at the time of his death.

Charlton C. Jernigan, President of Queens College, Charlotte, North Carolina, on the 22nd July.

Elliott Crayton McCants, editor, farmer, author, teacher, for many years (1907–1945) superintendent of city schools in Anderson, North Carolina, in October.

Robert Lee Ramsay, Professor of English in the University of Missouri, on the 14th December, his seventy-third birthday. Professor Ramsay wrote a foreword to F. G. Cassidy's "The Place Names of Dane County, Wisconsin" (*PADS*, No. 7) and was the author of "The Place Names of Boone County, Missouri" (*PADS*, No. 18).

F. THE SOUTH ATLANTIC REGIONAL DIVISION

The South Atlantic Regional Division met in Chattanooga, Tennessee, November 28, 1953, with the South Atlantic Modern Language Association. Gordon R. Wood presided, and papers were read by Hennig Cohen ("A Colonial Topographical Poem"), Thomas Pyles ("Some Observations on American Dialect Origins"), Sumner Ives ("Did Uncle Remus Talk Like That?"), and James B. McMillan ("Progress on Two Dictionaries of American English: Dialect and Usage"). Ernest H. Cox and Hennig Cohen were elected Chairman and Secretary, respectively, for 1954.

THOMAS PYLES
Secretary-Treasurer

THE AMERICAN DIALECT SOCIETY

Membership is conferred upon any person interested in the aims and activities of the Society. Dues for regular members (persons and institutions) are $3 a year; for contributing members, $5 (or more) a year. Members receive free all publications. The price of any one issue when purchased separately will depend upon the production cost of that issue.

The *Publication of the American Dialect Society* is issued twice a year, in April and November.